# Fly-Fishing the

# Texas Hill Country

A Guide to Fishing & Lodging on Thirteen Texas Rivers

by B.L. "Bud" Priddy

1994 Edition

AUSTIN ∾ W. THOMAS TAYLOR

*Published by*

W. THOMAS TAYLOR, INC.

1906 Miriam, Austin, Texas 78722

512-478-7628 FAX 478-5508

Cover and title-page illustrations by
Barbara Whitehead.

# TABLE OF CONTENTS

## THE RIVERS

## Publisher's Note

Bud Priddy, who was raised in Camp Wood, Texas, on the Nueces River, has been fishing the streams of Central Texas for more than thirty years, and he knows the lore of these streams better than most anyone. Dog-eared copies of a small xeroxed version of his guide, issued by the Alamo Fly Fishers in San Antonio in 1987, circulate among those who have discovered the pleasures of fishing the lovely, uncrowded waters of the Hill Country. We are pleased to make this greatly expanded and refined version available to the public.

This is the first edition of what will always be a work in progress. We plan to issue a new edition every two years, incorporating changes, corrections, and additions that we have discovered or that have been brought to our attention by users of the guide. *Please send us any corrections or suggestions you might have* — it will help make the next edition better. (We already have plans to include in the next edition an essay by Bud Priddy on the history of fishing on Texas rivers; a section on public ponds in Central Texas; more on white bass fishing by Joe Robinson; and a section on the Colorado River between Austin and Smithville.)

This guide does not contain maps, for the simple reason that it is impractical to create maps on a small scale that are accurate enough to include all of the country road crossings that are important to access on these rivers. Thus the guide was designed to be used with *The Roads of Texas*, a comprehensive atlas of Texas roads that can be found in most bookstores. The beginning of each river description tells which pages of *The Roads of Texas* should be consulted for detailed guidance.

We hope that this guide will lead you to many a fine day of fishing on these streams—and we would only ask, as Bud Priddy does several times in the text, that you help keep the streamsides clean by carrying out your trash (and that of others as well), and that you practice catch-and-release fishing, to help maintain a healthy population of sport fish in waters that do not receive constant stocking by the state.

The author and publisher would like to thank the following people for their assistance in preparing this guide: Dudley Sanford, Pete Jones, Irving O'Neil, David Young, Rod Staggs, Ray Box, Larry Sunderland, Joe Robinson, and Bill Jones. The publisher would also like to offer this book to the fond memory of Fred Whitehead, a Texas angler who loved these streams.

## A Word of Caution About Access

This book is about fishing; it is not an attempt to address Texas law regarding the definition of, access to, or proper utilization of public waters. No one contributing to the book can, or does, imply any guarantee as to the legality of any particular manner or means of entrance to a river at an access point. The question of legal access to the rivers of Texas is often unclear. If you desire to enter private property in order to fish a certain portion of a river, first seek and obtain permission from the owner. Each fly-fisher should uphold good sportsmanship and conduct when on or adjacent to a private landowner's property and should observe any fenced or posted areas. Respect the property of others and enjoy the fine fly-fishing opportunities offered by our area rivers.

# Prologue

This book was conceived and written with the purpose of introducing a fly-fisher to the unique and often excellent fly-fishing opportunities available in our Texas Hill Country streams. Guadalupe bass and sunfish catches can be outstanding. The largemouth and smallmouth fishing is excellent in some areas.

Central Texas has long been famous for its beauty and for the hunting of native and exotic game. Its history is varied and fascinating, as this area of Texas has been occupied by humans for some eight to ten thousand years. Evidence of human activity in the remote past can be found along many of the streams we will discuss. There are rock middens on the banks of some of these streams where one can find artifacts created by prehistoric peoples. One can visit Spanish missions and old forts that housed calvary detachments. Spanish mine shafts have been exposed by wind and rain along the canyon walls. These were gold and silver mines. Historic markers where cattle herds were crossed on their way to Kansas are found at some access points along the rivers. This is a bird watcher's paradise, with many varieties of birds, in great flocks, calling this area home. In the spring, the Texas Hill Country is the cradle for thousands of acres of wildflowers.

Access to these rivers is most easily achieved by using state and county road crossings, which can give potential access to all the streams in Texas that are navigable. Legal access to our rivers in Texas is unclear. Some additional thoughts on this will be noted later.

Deer hunting is a tradition in Central Texas in the late fall and becomes an obsession with some people. This would be the most likely time of the year to have a confrontation with a landowner or hunter. If you fish in November or December, I recommend that you fish for trout on the Guadalupe below Canyon Dam. Otherwise, you might find yourself gazing over the end of a pickup bed with your tongue hanging out. In any case, our native bass and sunfish become sluggish and difficult to catch from November to April, and fishing the Hill Country streams isn't very productive during that time. The exception to this is the runs of white bass that occur in the spring. The fishing for spawning white bass can be excellent in the early spring and is discussed in the section dealing with the Colorado River.

I hope this book will provide you with the information needed to fish this area and with the impetus to get out and scout around. That's half the fun! Let me leave you with one last thought before we begin: "Knowledge is a treasure but practice is the key to it!"

## The Streams

These rivers arise in deep canyons that darken early. It has been suggested that the native peoples in the farthest reaches of the canyons use owls for roosters. It is true that some families, in the recent past, came to town only once per month.

The streams are generally crystal clear at their origins due to flow from springs in their upper regions. John Gierach once commented, "You can count the scales on a bluegill in ten feet of water!" when referring to the clarity of the water in the upper Nueces River near Camp Wood, Texas. The rivers turn to a hazy murkiness as they progress into the southern and southeastern regions of the Hill Country on their journey to the Gulf of Mexico. The eastern Hill Country streams — the Lampasas, the San Gabriel, and the Colorado — have a rich greenness much like the streams of East and East Central Texas. The Nueces and the Frio remain cool in July and August, while other streams tend to heat up. This is apparently due to spring flow along the course of these rivers. Carp spawning activity in the spring can create cloudiness, which doesn't interfere with a stream's fishability, though it does reduce the esthetics of the experience somewhat.

The native peoples have devised some rather ingenious means of gathering fish, such as telephone cranks, dynamite, 30-30 rifles, etc. One of the more novel ideas is to rope carp with copper wire. They attach a length of copper wire to a cane pole, create a loop in the end of the wire, and move the loop up behind the pectoral fins of a carp resting near the bottom of the river. A quick jerk results in a roped carp that is hoisted out on the bank. Needless to say this requires significant water clarity as well as a good set of nerves.

Carp can be caught on nymphs. This will occasionally occur on the Guadalupe River during fishing for trout. Crayfish patterns are reputed to be quite good for carp as well. I have tried to catch large carp on the Pedernales River with crayfish patterns but have been unsuccessful. This is probably fortunate for my tackle.

Dr. Charles Mims, of San Antonio, has caught a couple of large longnosed gars on fly rods while fishing the Llano River. For a while, there was some question as to who had caught whom. This is an inadvisable activity unless you have some long-nosed pliers or a hemostat.

There are large numbers of catfish in these rivers. An occasional catch will be made on a woolly-bugger or some other deep-running fly, fished very slowly. Ounce for ounce, the catfish is probably king of all fighting fish in these rivers. The only thing that might come close would be a gar or a carp.

The prize catch on these streams is the northern largemouth, but small-mouth bass are beginning to appear on many of these streams. The largest bass we have personally seen come out of one of these rivers was said to weigh just over twelve pounds. It had a huge mouth. A large man's arm could easily pass through that maw. This fish was caught almost fifty years ago by an old man using a throw line and a large minnow.

There are occasional reports of very large fish being caught, but these invariably occur after heavy rains and most likely represent fish from stock tanks that were released by flood waters into the rivers. The Florida largemouth reaches double-digit weights in stock tanks but does very poorly in stream environments. The native northern largemouths have made a dramatic comeback in the rivers since the decrease in number of fish that may be kept and the increased legal size on keepers. Before many of the dams were built, there was heavy stocking of the rivers by the state. There is very infrequent stocking now, but since we have more spawning-size fish due to the new regulations, our fishing has rebounded.

The rivers covered are bounded by the Llano to the west, the Lampasas to the east, and the San Saba to the north. An argument could be advanced that the Devil's River should be included since it lies on the fringe of the Hill Country. This river is excellent for smallmouth bass that have ascended the river from Lake Amistad. Access is a problem! Baker's Crossing, on highway 163 south of Juno, Texas, is the only access point where one can fish and camp easily. There is a trailer park and a small store for supplies at Juno. The phone number for Baker's Crossing is 915-292-4503.

It is unfortunate that these rivers have been trashed so badly. We would like to suggest you take a trash bag along for each person in your party. Fill them as you fish by boat or after you fish if wade fishing. We believe this will help to preserve the few remaining access points by defusing some of the natural anger felt by the landowners.

## *Sport Fish Found in Hill Country Streams*

There are four bass species available — northern largemouth, spotted bass, Guadalupe bass, and smallmouth bass. The first three are native species. The smallmouth were introduced into lakes and have made their way upstream from the reservoirs. They occur in stream systems that have impoundments along their course, such as the San Saba, Guadalupe, Llano, and Devil's rivers.

The spotted, Guadalupe, and smallmouth all tend to hold in swifter water than the largemouth, at least in their smaller sizes. The larger of these three species tend to move toward shade and cover along the banks as they increase in size.

The key to larger fish is to pound the banks and holes. A faster retrieve works for bass in stream situations. A leisurely fished fly will result in more strikes by sunfish. Keep the rod tip down and use the non-rod hand to strip line. This gives you a much greater chance of setting the hook in a large bass. Holding the rod high, as in trout fishing, results in many lost fish. Most bass will attempt to slug it out at close quarters. Stumps, rocks, etc., are not a big problem in these streams from the standpoint of losing a fish that has fouled the line around an obstruction. Because of this, it is much easier to get a fish on the reel. However, you must not give a big bass slack, or you will lose it. The lack of spots where one is likely to foul the line results in an angler's ability to use light tackle in these streams with success. A four- or five-weight rod is adequate for most situations but does present problems when casting larger flies. If one were limited to one rod, a six-weight would be the most practical for bass and trout. I tend to gravitate to eight-weight if I am trying to catch large bass. The reason for this is the ease in casting large hair bugs, not an inability to handle the larger bass with a small rod. I have landed eight-pound bass on a four/five-weight rod using a five-weight line.

There are seven species of sunfish found in Hill Country streams. These include Rio Grande perch, rock bass, bluegills, green, yellow-belly, red ear, and long ear sunfish.

The Rio Grande perch is very powerful, and the males will approach one pound in weight. They are great on light tackle. The only problem is they are not inclined to hit a fly. One will occasionally catch a Rio Grande on a popping bug. These fish travel in schools, and if one will strike, others can sometimes be induced to hit.

Red ears will take popping bugs in the spring. The males will frequently weigh close to a pound. The females will average about a half pound. The takes are explosive, and they will fight hard when hooked. During the summer and fall, the red ears will take streamers and nymphs fished near the bottom.

Long ears, also known as cherry bream, are rare. I have caught only one in over thirty years of fishing on Hill Country streams. They are the most beautiful of all the sunfish but tend to be small.

Rock bass, also known locally as goggle-eyes, are explosive hitters on surface lures but tire quickly. It's great fun to bounce an Arkansas Hair Fly off a rock next to a deep hole and have rock bass smash it time after time. Their splashy rise makes up for the lack of stamina. The average size is about a half pound.

Green sunfish are similar to rock bass in their smashing hits at surface lures. Unfortunately, they also tire easily. You will still enjoy them on light tackle. The green sunfish take streamers, nymphs, and popping bugs readily. The larger males will weigh about three-quarters of a pound.

Yellow-belly sunfish are great fly rod quarry. They have lots of stamina, grow larger than the average sunfish, and the bigger ones will take surface lures from early spring right through the fall. The yellow-belly sunfish occur in good numbers on most of our streams but do not tend to overpopulate and produce runts like the bluegills do. (This also does not seem to occur with the other five species of sunfish.) Yellow-belly sunfish will take popping bugs, streamers, and nymphs with great enthusiasm.

The bluegill is the most widespread and most prevalent sunfish in our streams. Unfortunately, this has resulted in a tendency to produce runt fish due to poor food supplies. This tendency to overpopulate is most apparent on the Frio River. The largest bluegills come to a fly fished deep such as a nymph or small streamer. A Girdle Bug or Bitch Creek nymph will bring up some eye openers. Bluegills will take popping bugs and dry flies readily, but the average size will be considerably smaller than those caught near the bottom. Occasionally, you will find areas where the current is swift and there are deep holes gouged in the river bottom that will hold large fish. These bluegills will attack popping bugs with violent, slashing strikes.

## What's Available for the Fish

There is a full pantry of types of foods available for the fish, from large meat forms such as minnows and crayfish, to dainty mayflies. There are "Spot Tail Shiners," "Red Shiners," and "Stonerollers" in large numbers. The bass also feed on their own young as well as sunfish fry. There is a small minnow called a "Potbelly Minnow" by the locals, which is probably a Flathead Minnow, that the bass work pretty heavily in the evenings. The locals call the Red Shiners "Red Horse Minnows." Stonerollers are known as "Sucker Minnows" since their mouths are on the bottom. One will find a few sculpin types, some very colorful, if searched for diligently.

Crayfish are quite common. There are at least three species in the Guadalupe system, a large red, a medium orange-brown, and a small dark olive. The red and green varieties occur in the other streams. Hellgrammites or Dobson fly larvae and Alder fly larvae are quite common. The hellgrammites are used for catfish bait by the canyon folk, especially on the Llano River. Dragonflies and damselflies are very common. Olive woolly-worms and woolly-buggers work very well for both bass and sunfish, most likely due to the large numbers of these nymphs in these waters. Check low-water bridge abutments for shed skins of these nymphs. You will be surprised at the large numbers you will find.

There are trillions of midges in these rivers. Try taking a lantern to the edge of a stream after dark. Light it and step back several feet lest you near suffocate from midges up your nose and in your mouth. There are several mayfly types, representing all categories such as swimmers, burrowers, clingers, and crawlers, in these rivers. It's interesting to see sunfish become selective to a mayfly hatch such as Tricos but at other times completely ignore other large mayflies.

## A Word About Technique for Bass and Sunfish

The old cliché "Big Flies — Big Fish!" certainly applies to some extent on these rivers. Almost all of the big fish (over three pounds) caught will be taken on large flies such as a Dahlberg Diver, Dave's Swimming Frog, Joe's Mud Bug, or Dave's Hare Water Pup. Therefore, you must decide whether to use large flies and catch fewer but larger fish, or to use small flies and catch dozens of smaller fish. Good-sized Guadalupe bass and yellow-belly perch will also take large lures. It's just more fun to fish for several hours with a four- or five-weight outfit as opposed to a seven- or eight-weight. A lot easier on the arm! We are talking twenty or thirty fish versus a hundred fish in a day if one uses smaller lures. It's great fun to catch half-pound Guadalupe bass and yellow-belly perch on small sliders and popping bugs.

I recommend Dave Whitlock's technique for bass bugs. Use a sink-tip line with the first five feet removed and a short (about four-foot) leader. These fish are not leader shy! Bass tend to respond to a fast retrieve in these streams, but do vary the rhythm of your retrieve. Watch the frogs and minnows jump from spot to spot as they flee from a pursuing bass. They seem to hardly enter the water before they are airborne again. The sunfish seem to be attracted to a more leisurely fished lure. I have caught bass that struck a lead weight being dragged along the bottom of a river on a throw line. Apparently it looks to a hungry bass like a crayfish scooting through the muck on the bottom. Experiment! Don't get in a rut! Bass will respond to a variety of presentations, even a lure just floating quietly.

Here's a list of the various types of lures I have found effective for bass and sunfish:

### Streamers
1. Woolly Bugger – olive, black, olive and black
2. Light Edson Tiger
3. Dark Edson Tiger
4. Muddler Minnow
5. Bloody Muddler
6. Mickey Finn
7. Black Nosed Dace
8. Zonkers – various colors
9. Platte River Special with a red head
10. Marabou Streamers – various colors

### Poppers and Sliders
1. Bass Duster
2. Sneaky Pete
3. Pencil Poppers
4. Peck's Minnow
5. Hula Poppers
6. Miss Prissy
7. Minnie Pop
8. Dixie Devil
9. Ol' Joe

### Bass Flies – Surface
1. Dave's Swimming Frogs
2. Dave's Deer Hair Bugs – various colors
3. Dahlberg Divers – various colors
4. Dahlberg Sliders – various colors
5. Dave's Hopper
6. Ugly Rudamus
7. Madame X
8. Goddard Caddis

### Bass Flies – Subsurface
1. Hare Water Pup
2. Hare Water Dog
3. Joe's Mud Bug
4. Clouser's Crayfish
5. Whit's Eelworm Streamer
6. Shinabou Shiner in yellow
7. Clouser's Minnow
8. Clouser's Deep Minnow

I do not recommend using a float tube to float from access point to access point. It is unlikely, but you could get a foot caught in a crevice in the river bottom and be dragged under. Also, a float tube is simply impractical on streams with long stretches of fairly thin water. Use the tube to fish the large holes and small lakes found on these streams. Use a canoe or some other shallow-draft craft to float between access points. This is much safer and much less tiring when fishing over six to eight hours. Be alert! Large bass will almost always go upstream on their first run after being hooked. This results in many lost fish if the canoe can't be stopped or turned while you fight the fish. It is difficult to keep a tight line while turning in a canoe to fight a fish that is going the other way.

## Potential Aggravations or Dangers

These Hill Country streams are hazardous if not given proper respect. Runoff from flash floods can be extremely dangerous. Almost every year someone is killed while trying to cross a low-water crossing during a flood. The water can rise quickly and unexpectedly, miles downstream from heavy rains, where the fisherman is experiencing only a drizzle.

I have seen the Nueces River on thirty-five-foot rises at Camp Wood. It is awesome to see pecan trees that are one hundred feet tall jerked out of the ground and floated down the river. One has only to look at the huge stumps of cypress trees that have been snapped off along the Medina and Guadalupe rivers to gain respect for the potential hazards generated by flood waters. It is also interesting to visit familiar areas on a stream and see how the character of the river has changed due to shifting of gravel bars by flood waters.

At the other extreme is the frequent loss of flow due to prolonged periods of drought, which occur fairly regularly in the Hill Country. This is semi-arid country, and the rivers are subject to low flows. *Before you plan a float on a river be sure the flow is adequate.* One would not wish to carry a canoe for any great distance between water holes. This does tend to concentrate the fish but also puts a premium on long, delicate casts to prevent spooking the fish in the holes left as the river goes under the gravel. I suspect birds and coons give the fish fits under these low-water conditions and make the fish more wary of any potential danger.

Please keep in mind that many of the longer floats described in this book pass through large ranches and relatively uninhabited country. If you have a problem, it may take some hiking to get help—so be careful, and before setting out consult a map so that in the event of trouble you will have a good sense of which direction to take for assistance. It is advisable to take two or more crafts on each float due to possible disability to one, even on short or familiar stretches of these rivers.

Animals present a problem at times. Bulls in pastures along the stream can be a problem, but cows can be extremely aggressive as well. Be especially wary of wild animals that have been made into pets. I have seen a nose sliced open by the hoof of a pet doe. Buck deer can become very aggressive in the fall, and people have been killed by bucks in the rut.

Rabid animals are not unusual in this area. Rabid foxes have attacked people in Camp Wood. A rabid skunk bit an illegal alien near Rocksprings. The man did not seek medical attention and died with rabies. I have had personal experience in treating an individual who was attacked by a rabid bobcat at Garner State Park and several men who were exposed to a rabid cow. They thought the cow had a bone stuck in her throat and all ran their hands down her throat. They were exposed through cuts on their hands. This occurred near Uvalde, Texas. Beware anytime you are approached by a wild animal. This is not normal behavior. Skunks are very nearsighted and will occasionally come close because they don't see you, but the best approach to near contact with a wild animal is to quit the area.

All four of the poisonous snakes found in Texas inhabit this area. The most dangerous is the western diamondback rattler due to its large size and the amount of venom injected. Rattlesnakes can swim and have been seen in these rivers on rare occasions. There are some six foot rattlers out there so be careful. If bitten, pack the limb in ice if available and head for town.

The cottonmouth does occur but is quite unusual. We know of only one bite by a cottonmouth. This occurred on Pulliam Creek, north of Camp Wood. Others undoubtedly have occurred but are rare compared to rattlesnake bites.

The copperhead is unlikely to be encountered unless you plow around in caves or in leaf piles along a stream. These are very reclusive snakes and are not very aggressive.

An adult has little to fear from a coral snake. Their mouths are small, and they would have to get you in the web between your fingers or toes. They also have to chew to inject venom. Not too many of us are going to stand still for that. These are very non-aggressive snakes, and there have been stories of people carrying them around for hours without being bitten.

## Legal Access to Rivers
by David Young

Years ago when I joined the Alamo Fly Fishers one of the first things I was asked to do was write part of the prologue for our booklet on fly-fishing area rivers. Everyone was concerned about legal access to the rivers, and since I had admitted to being guilty of being an attorney, the thought was I should say something on the subject. My original words are paraphrased on page 6 of the present book.

Since those words were written, I have overheard and tried not to get involved in several conversations with different members concerning river access for fishing. I've tried to stay out of those discussions due to a sense of professional caution; I don't want anyone to think I told them it was all right for them to go do whatever it is they might end up doing on someone else's property adjacent to a river.

Even so, there are some basic principles involved in the public ownership of many rivers in Texas. Be forewarned, however, that the following generalizations about Texas law are not intended as legal advice about any particular factual situation that may arise in the future.

Perhaps the most basic principle of Texas law in this area is that the state usually retains title to the bed of all navigable streams. There are certain exceptions to this rule, mostly going back to early Mexican land grants (where the stream bed sometimes was conveyed in the grant) and other situations where the state may have transferred title itself. Both are rare instances. In fact, it is unlawful for a surveyor to run a survey line across a navigable stream, so there's essentially no way for someone to claim title to the bed of a navigable stream based on a lawful survey. If the survey shows he owns the navigable stream bed by virtue of a survey line that crosses the bed, the survey itself is illegal. You would have to do a title search on each piece of property in question to begin to figure this stuff out, and the answer you get might still not be correct because of other laws outside of the limited scope of this article.

Not only does the state own the stream bed, it reserves to itself and the public the natural resources located in the bed, and by implication the necessary and accompanying rights of ingress and egress to those resources, and all other rights necessary to their proper use and development. Fish are such natural resources and fishing is a lawful and permitted activity.

If you're following this, by now you should have asked yourself, "What is a navigable stream anyway?" The legal definition of a navigable stream is a stream that retains an average width of thirty feet from the mouth up to the point at which the question arises, that is, from the mouth to wherever you want to fish and someone else claims you can't because they own it. Legal navigability has nothing to do with actual navigability. It doesn't matter if the water is only three-eighths of an inch deep or even if there are places where sometimes during the year there's no water at all. Better yet, a stream can become navigable even if it wasn't so when the original land patents were issued. If a stream meanders, that is, changes course, the new stream bed also becomes public.

Islands formed in a navigable stream belong to the state as well; however, if the island was formed by a meandering stream that cuts off land from a landowner, the landowner still owns the island even though he may have lost title to the new stream bed in the process.

So far this has been simple, so let's see if we can't confuse the issue some. Try this idea on for size: Even though the title to a stream bed can belong to a landowner, the stream can still meet the definition of a navigable stream. Even if a landowner has the right to maintain and use dams on the river, those rights do not keep the stream from being legally navigable. Consider that alongside the right of the public to use a navigable stream for any lawful purpose. One thing that is clear is that the right to fish does not authorize trespass to reach the navigable stream and its fish.

Your next question should be "Where's the boundary line between the public and the private land?" Unfortunately, the line isn't drawn on the ground for all to see. Neither is it necessarily where the private landowner happens to put a fence. In fact, it's almost certainly not where the fence gets put. The legal definition of the boundary line is that it is a gradient of the flowing water of the stream. That gradient is located midway between the lower level of the flowing water that just reaches the cut bank and the higher level of it that just does not overtop the cut bank. In other words, the line is a point half the distance between the top and the bottom of the cut bank, no matter how high or low the water actually is on a given day. If you picture the situation in your mind where the river is high and near the top of the cut bank, you'll see that virtually all the public land is under water. However, if you imagine a low river, you can picture many points of land and bars that would be in the public domain even though they may be directly connected to the private owner's land.

There's been a lot of litigation in Texas concerning public and private ownership in this area. Most of the court cases are not about fishing, although some certainly are, but they all have to do with navigable streams. Remember, if it's navigable, we can fish it! But don't get yourself shot trying.

## More About Access

What is permissible access and what is trespass is obviously confusing and subject to local interpretation. Several years ago a rancher in Uvalde County brought a local man to trial for trespass when the individual was caught deer hunting on the Nueces River. The man was in the river bed, and a county judge ruled the man was not trespassing because the state streams belong to the people of the state of Texas. Another judge might well have found the man guilty.

We strongly recommend that you seek permission before entering private property. You should conduct yourself politely when on or adjacent to private property. Do not violate fenced or posted areas. If you can be sure the access point is used by local people, there is less likelihood there will be problems. Unfortunately, the most reliable sign of local use is trash littering the banks.

Floating seems less likely to cause a confrontation. Presumably, this is due to the fact that you are encroaching on the river bottom infrequently, if at all. If you want to float between access points and there is no commercial shuttle service available, a stop at a local service station or garage and an offer of $10 for a shuttle of you and your craft to a point upstream a few miles will often meet with a friendly response.

The older farm and ranch families are much less likely to confront you along a stream. In fact, they will often stop to chat and give advice about good fishing spots. Non-resident ownership of farms and ranches along rivers and the building of summer homes or retirement homes on small plots of land adjacent to the rivers tend to aggravate access problems. The Blanco, Medina, Frio, and upper Guadalupe rivers are good examples of where this has happened. However, even here a courteous request will frequently pave the way for an enjoyable outing.

We can expect more problems with access to occur as the population of Texas increases and more people attempt to utilize the river resources. *Ask permission to enter a river when it is possible to do so and conduct yourself in a manner that brings honor upon our sport of fly-fishing.* Doing these things, and carrying away your trash, plus a bit of trash left behind by someone else, will go a long way toward ensuring a welcome the next time you arrive at a river.

# *Blanco River*

FOUND ON PAGES 129 AND 119 OF THE ROADS OF TEXAS

The Blanco River is a small stream that has some excellent fishing — but access is somewhat limited. This is unfortunate since this river contains some big largemouth, Guadalupe, and smallmouth bass.

The river flows out of Kendall County into Blanco County and eventually into Hays County, where it joins the San Marcos River. There is only one access in Kendall County that is worth mentioning, and that is very limited due to trespass potential. This is a dirt road off FM 1880 west of Blanco, Texas, that crosses the river. The river is shallow between the small holes created by dams until it arrives at Blanco State Park. There is considerable water available in the park, and the sunfish fishing should be good with nymphs fished deep.

**River Mile 0** The first access of interest to us is in Blanco County, east of Blanco, Texas, where FM 2325 and RR 165 cross the river. Fishing is not possible above, but one may walk downstream for wade fishing. There is some local use for swimming, so landowner problems are minimal. A new bridge is being built here that may affect access. Take CR 404 to the right under the bridge and park under the trees about 200 yards from the bridge.

**River Mile 1.75** This is the CR 405 crossing off RR 165. Parking is available. There is some potential for good catches of bass and sunfish.

**River Mile 5** This is the CR 406 crossing between RR 32 and RR 165. Park on the northeast side of the river. There is some wade fishing downstream for sunfish and some larger-than-average bass. This would be a good take-out for a float from Mile 0; it would require portage over two small dams but would place the floaters over some very large bass.

**River Mile 6.5** This is the CR 407 crossing off RR 165. This is called Chimney Valley Road. This offers potential for access or for take-out. Parking is not possible.

**River Mile 8** This is the second crossing by CR 407 as it returns to RR 2325, just south of RR 165 intersection. Again, there is a problem with parking. Potential take-out for float from above.

**River Mile 21.25** This is the FM 181 crossing at Fisher, Texas. This is called Pleasant Valley Road Crossing, and it was indeed once a pleasant spot. The old low-water bridge has now been replaced by a high bridge, however, and the scenic and angling qualities of this crossing are much diminished. Access is no longer possible. For reasons of safety (people are killed every year trying to cross low-water bridges on rivers in flood) the state is more or less systematically putting in new high bridges on rivers in Texas. Do not be surprised if other access points noted in this book disappear over the next few years, as this trend continues.

**River Mile 30.75** This is the CR 178 crossing west of Wimberley, Texas. This road leaves FM 2325 on the northern outskirts of Wimberley. This is known as Cloptin's Crossing. This is another access point that is no longer available, in this case because of development. The new resort that borders the river has posted the banks and apparently will tow anyone who parks along the river.

**River Mile 33.25** This access is in Hays County southeast of Wimberley. It is reached by taking FM 3237 off RR 12 to the north. Take a right on CR 173, and park. Then walk down to the stream on CR 314.

**River Mile 34.25** Take CR 174 off CR 173 and go to the opposite side of the river for access. Good fishing for sunfish and bass in the lake above the crossing. Follow CR 174 beyond the third crossing to Little Arkansas campground, which is quite nice and offers fishing in the river. The best fishing occurs 1/2 mile downstream, for smallmouths and average-sized sunfish.

**River Mile 44.75** This is Dudley Johnson Park, a county park southwest of Kyle, Texas. This is a good take-out for a float from near Wimberley, a distance of about 11 1/2 miles. There is excellent access in the park to a small lake that holds some large bass.

**River Mile 50** There is a county road crossing between Kyle and San Marcos that is difficult to locate. From I-35 take exit 110 (Yarrington Road). Turn left over the interstate and go to CR 140. Take a left and go a mile or so to the crossing. From this crossing you can follow CR 136 to the county park in Kyle — a nice drive. If you get lost, ask directions locally. May be a potential take-out for a float from the county park, a distance of about 5 miles.

**River Mile 52** This is the I-35 crossing northeast of San Marcos. There is good access for above-average sunfish and small bass.

**River Mile 55.5** This is the CR 295 crossing southeast of San Marcos just above the union of the Blanco and the San Marcos rivers. This is reached by going south on SH 80, turning right on CR 101, and taking an almost immediate right on CR 295. Very good access for small bass and some average sunfish. Some wading is possible here, but it is best floated.

## Food & Lodging on the Blanco

In Blanco, Texas, the Sunset Restaurant is quite good. For Mexican food, try the Rio Blanco Restaurant. Swiss Lodge (210-833-5528) is a new and pleasant motel in Blanco. Camping is available at the Blanco State

Park. They have screened shelters, RV sites, and tent camping sites. Call 210-833-4333. The Amenehal Bed and Breakfast establishment is available in Blanco at 210-833-5438.

In Wimberley, Texas, the Mountain View Motel is available at 512-847-2992. Seven Oaks Resort at Wood Creek is nice but may be somewhat expensive, since they cater to meetings. Their number is 512-847-3126. Try Hill Country Accommodations, 1-800-926-5028; Wimberley Lodging, 1-800-460-3909, and Bed and Breakfasts of Wimberley for bed and breakfasts, condos, cabins, etc. Camping is available at The Blue Hole, 512-847-9127. Adequate restaurants include Casa Blanca, Cypress Creek Cafe, John Henry's, and the Golden Spoon.

In San Marcos try Fuschak's Pit Bar-B-Q or Palmer's Restaurant and Bar. The Crystal River Inn is a bed-and-breakfast establishment at 512-396-3739. Good motels include the Holiday Inn, 512-353-8011; Days Inn, 512-353-5050; and the Stratford House Inn at 512-396-3700.

# Colorado River

## by Joe Robinson

FOUND ON PAGE 101 OF THE ROADS OF TEXAS

The white bass (*maron chrysops*), also known as sand bass in the northern part of the state and sometimes as white perch in East Texas, is often overlooked as a suitable game fish for fly-fishers. In fact, just a few articles have been written about fishing for them in any of the prominent fly-fishing magazines in the last twenty years. This is probably because most of the year this "cool water" fish is resident in deeper water in reservoirs, and most fly-fishermen resist using high-density sinking lines to get a fly down to them. Primarily a baitfish feeder, the white bass hunts in large schools chasing threadfin and gizzard shad and minnows all over the lake.

The good news for fly-fishers is that in the late winter and early spring white bass begin to move into shallow water to spawn, and this puts them well within the range of most fly-fishers armed with a floating line. Depending on weather patterns and temperature levels, this spawning urge draws schools of male white bass into shallow "staging areas," usually in late January or early February in Central Texas, as they eagerly await the arrival of the females. White bass can spawn in practically any part of the lake that has a clean, shallow, sandy or fine-gravel bottom, and where wave action provides plenty of oxygen. They seem to prefer tributaries with moving water, or tailraces below dams.

The Central Texas Hill Country is one of the best areas in the state for outstanding white bass "runs," and there is probably no better place to be found than the upper Colorado River above Lake Buchanan. This big lake, 60 miles above Austin, has throughout its history been a premiere white bass fishery because of the rich alkalinity of the Colorado River water and the sandy-rocky nature of the river bottom, which provides perfect spawning areas. The river bed is state owned for 75 miles above Lake Buchanan, providing unlimited wading opportunities. Of primary interest to the fly-rodder are a series of privately owned fishing camps and a state park located just past the tiny town of Bend, Texas. Bend is located about 20 miles out of Lampasas on SH 580, on the banks of the Colorado. The camps are easy to find once you reach the town of Bend; just follow the signs down a long gravel-and-dirt road. The camps and state park welcome fishermen from the first of February through April for the white bass runs.

The park is located on the old Lemmons ranch property at the junction of the Colorado River and Lake Buchanan. Because of its proximity to the lake, this is a good place to start fishing in early February. There are shallow sections of the river that can be waded, and float-tube fishers and canoeists can fish the deeper water with sinking lines. Striped bass are often hooked in this deeper water, where the white bass begin their staging prior to moving into the river. This is a primitive state park with almost no facilities, and usually it is not open until February 1 for fishing. Automobiles must be parked at the entrance, and all travel is limited to hiking.

Adjacent to the state park is another large tract of state land on the

Colorado purchased in the early 1980s. This land includes Gorman Falls, a favorite fishing camp among devoted white bass fishermen for many, many years. However, for reasons known only to our state officials, this camp has been closed to the public ever since the purchase. Because the Colorado is a state-owned riverbed, Gorman Falls can still be fished by boat or by wading, just be darn sure you don't walk on any part of the bank that has grass on it (according to the Texas Parks and Wildlife), or you will be given a ticket for being out of the stream bed.

Moving up the river, the next camp is a beautiful privately owned 4-mile stretch of water called Sulphur Springs. A lot more water is available to the wade fisher here than at the state park. A road parallels the river along most of the property. Camping is permitted, and fishing can be outstanding along this stretch during March and early April.

The last camp up the river is Barefoot Camp, which also gets runs of white bass; in fact, white bass are caught as far up the river as the highway bridge at Bend. The camps and the state park charge a nominal day fee for fishing, or an overnight camping fee.

White bass are primarily bait-fish feeders, and when they're in the river a major part of their diet is small river minnows, leeches, and crayfish. Popular lures for light and ultralight spinning tackle (the preferred equipment for most folks fishing the run) are small 1/32-, 1/16-, or 1/8-ounce jigs. These jigs are often suspended by floats to keep them from hanging in the rocky crevasses along the bottom. The fly-rodder's favorite flies are minnow imitations or streamers in hook sizes 6 through 12. The important thing is that the patterns be tied on hooks that are equipped with a snag guard, or tied so that they run hook up in jig fashion; otherwise the angler will be constantly hanging up on the bottom and losing flies. Micro jigs are available in some fly shops in the 1/124 ounce and 1/80 ounce sizes and work great.

White bass feed almost always on or near the bottom of the river, and it is imperative to keep the fly working deep. For much of this section of the Colorado the depth can be as shallow as 2 feet to as deep as 6 feet during a year of normal rain. For this reason, successful fly-rodders will probably need a sinking or sinking-tip line to complement their floating line. This is particularly true in early February, when fish will be concentrated in deeper holes. When water temperatures rise above 60 degrees, more fish will be in shallower water.

Fly rods designed to cast 4- through 7-weight lines can be used, but because the wind can be really strong through this canyon area, a 6- or 7-weight outfit would be a better choice if the fly-rodder is limited to one rod.

Waders are required equipment this time of year, and an extra change of clothing will come in handy if you take a spill. This is not an easy river to wade because of the unpredictability of the rugged bottom and the murkiness of the water. It is very easy to trip over a rock or step into a hole and lose your balance. Unless the fly-rodder wades carefully and shuffles his feet slowly, he can be in for a very rough and wet day.

Fly-fishers who are most successful cover a lot of water. The fish are not everywhere and sometimes are not where they were found the year before, so keep moving. When fish are located, the "take" is often subtle. Retrieve the line with short, fairly rhythmic strips of 4 to 6 inches per strip, with the rod tip touching the water. Strike quickly at the slightest resistance of the fly. Some of the deeper water is better fished from a float tube. Besides white bass, the fly-rodder can expect to catch crappie, freshwater drum, black bass, sunfish, carp, catfish, an occasional striped bass and hybrid striped bass.

## Food & Lodging on the Colorado

The closest food and lodging, aside from the camps on the river, is in Lampasas — see listings under Lampasas River, page 43.

# *Frio River*

FOUND ON PAGE 127 OF THE ROADS OF TEXAS

The Frio originates in Real County and flows south into Uvalde County. The river becomes intermittent soon after leaving Con Can, Texas. Therefore, the upper river is of the most interest to us. The Frio is a very popular river and has hoards of tubers during the summer from May until after Labor Day weekend. In spite of the heavy traffic, there is still pretty good fishing for sunfish, especially green perch, which obtain good size. With some searching an occasional large bass can be caught in backwater areas. There are lots of small bluegills present all along the river.

This river has good flows in a normal year and is an excellent river for canoe travel. Dry spells will draw down the river considerably by September, and this should be taken into consideration when planning a trip. Because of the heavy use of the river by non-residents for tubing, the potential for landowner confrontation is high in areas other than the stretch between Garner State Park and Con Can. The best approach on this river appears to be to float between the various access points.

**River Mile 0** In Real County, FM 337 crosses the river 1 mile east of Leakey. There are very big green perch downstream and some very nice bass. Both sides of the river are owned by the same individuals, and they are very protective. They allow swimming near the bridge but will not allow wade fishing downstream. A good-sized pool above the bridge could be fished by canoe with a float back down to the bridge with a little extra effort.

**River Mile 2** This is the first RR 1120 crossing south of Leakey. Take RR 1120 to the east off US 83. This is a good take-out from the FM 337 crossing, or a launch site for a float to the second RR 1120 crossing. However, this area is highly developed with homes, and I don't recommend this float.

**River Mile 5** This is the RR 1120 crossing west of Rio Frio, Texas. Both crossings of RR 1120 are posted. Because of this we would recommend individuals float between FM 337 and the upper RR 1120 crossing only. This is about 2 miles by the river. You could safely use the second RR 1120 crossing as a launch site for a float to the RR 1050 crossing.

**River Mile 9** In Uvalde County, RR 1050 goes east off US 83 and crosses the river on its way to Utopia, Texas. There is fair to good fishing for bass and sunfish above the crossing. There are no posted signs and no fences blocking access. As indicated, this is a potential take-out for a float from the second crossing of RR 1120, about 4 river miles. A 1/2-mile walk downstream will bring you to fair fishing for bass and sunfish.

**River Mile 11** This is Garner State Park. The river is dammed in the park, and fishing is available, but the area is heavily fished, as you can imagine. This is a good launch site for a float downstream.

**River Mile 12** This is called Mager's Crossing. This access is reached by taking a dirt road off FM 1050 just after it crosses the river. Follow the dirt road south along the east side of the river as it runs parallel to the river. The dirt road eventually leads to US 83 after crossing the river south of Garner Park.

**River Mile 16** This is the crossing by CR 348. This road goes east off US 83. This is called Cliff Seven due to the markings on the cliff on the southwest side of the crossing. There is good fishing for bass and sunfish above the crossing. This is a good take-out or launch site for a float. CR 348 parallels the river on the east after crossing the river at Cliff Seven and eventually crosses again at Bee's Camp. There is no access at Bee's Camp except for campers. CR 348 enters Con Can from the north as it continues southwest.

**River Mile 20** SH 127 crosses the river at Con Can. This is the usual take-out point for tubers and canoe enthusiasts. The 4-mile float between Cliff Seven and Con Can is a good stretch of water, and there are a few bass and sunfish. There are also two small dams that require a portage in this stretch.

**River Mile 27.5** FM 2690 leaves SH 127 5 miles southeast of Con Can and crosses the river to the south. Currently there is a fence across the river both above and below the crossing. This is illegal but does indicate potential for a dispute with a landowner. Check to see if high water has taken the fences down. If that occurs, you can usually get access without problems to the waters above the crossing.

## Food & Lodging on the Frio

The Frio Canyon Restaurant in Leakey is quite adequate. There is a small barbecue restaurant in Leakey that is quite good. Ken's Country Kitchen about 2 1/2 miles north of Garner Park on US 83 is very good. Neal's Vacation Lodge and Restaurant in Con Can is also quite good. There are no good motels in the immediate area. One would need to locate in Uvalde. (See the list of motels for Uvalde given in the section about the Nueces River.) There is a bed-and-breakfast establishment called the Rio Frio B and B (210-232-6633) and another called the Whiskey Mountain Inn (210-232-6797).

There are many private camps up and down the river, but they tend to cease operation after Labor Day weekend. A good one is run by Edwin and Betty Niggli at Cliff Seven. Call 210-232-5581. Tent sites and RV parking are available. Their one cabin is rented many weeks in advance, so call very early. Try the Cliff Seven Cabins and RV Park next door at 210-232-5260 if you are not successful. Garner Park has screened shelters and overnight cabins, but these are also rented many weeks in advance. Call 210-232-6132. Crider's on US 83 is nice. Their number is 210-232-5584. Bee's Camp is a place to stay and gives access to the river for wade fishing. As indicated, this camp is north of Con Can on CR 348. All of these places fill in the summer, and you need to call for reservations early.

# Guadalupe River

FOUND ON PAGES 127 AND 128 OF THE ROADS OF TEXAS

The Guadalupe River is formed at Hunt, Texas, by the joining of the north and south forks. Both forks are highly developed with summer homes along their course. This results in a high probability of trespass accusations at access points. You must use extreme caution in this area. Ask permission if you have any doubts about the advisability of stopping at any point along these streams. This same problem exists on the main river, especially from Hunt to Ingram.

## North Fork

**River Mile 0** In Kerr County, the north fork begins at springs in the Kerr Wildlife Management Area. There are two designated fishing areas in the management area that give access. These areas are indicated by signs along RR 1340 between SH 41 and Hunt, Texas. These are very shallow and the fish are spooky, but this area is worth a look. Wading is prohibited.

**River Mile 9** This is a low-water bridge crossing on RR 1340 about 3 1/2 miles west of Hunt. There is a small dam on the river above the crossing. The plunge pool will usually contain some bass and good-sized sunfish.

**River Mile 9.5** This is a low-water bridge 3 1/4 miles west of Hunt on RR 1340 that is only recommended for a float to the next crossing about 2 miles downstream.

**River Mile 11.5** This is a low-water crossing on RR 1340 about 1 1/4 miles west of Hunt. There is some use by locals. There is some good bass and sunfish fishing above the crossing.

## South Fork

The south fork also arises in Kerr County. This branch is followed along its course by SH 39.

**River Mile 0** There is a low-water bridge about 7 1/2 miles southwest of Hunt on SH 39 that gives access. There are a large number of good sunfish and an occasional bass in the deeper holes if you look closely. This is undoubtedly private, but there are no signs, no fences, and no houses where you might ask permission.

**River Mile 1.75** The River Inn Resort sits on a lake behind a small dam built on the river. This is about 5 1/2 miles out of Hunt. Canoes are available to guests. The number is 210-238-4226. They would perhaps have information about other access points.

**River Mile 2.25**  About 5 miles southwest of Hunt on SH 39 is a bridge that gives access. There are no fences and no signs, but this would perhaps be a risky area. Local inquiry would be advisable. A canoe or float tube would be ideal.

## Main River

**River Mile 0**  About 1 river mile below Hunt on SH 39 is a crossing that is used by the locals for swimming. I have found an occasional good bass in the large pool below the crossing. The area above the crossing is not available.

**River Mile 4**  The next public access is New Lake Ingram. Wade fishing is possible for a short distance below the dam. A canoe, boat, or float tube would be ideal for the lake, which is small. There is a good access ramp for the lake 1/2 mile above the dam for the upper part of the lake, which has less motorboat traffic. Some sunfish and bass are available. For access to the river at this area we suggest the Waltonian Cabins (210-367-5613), which would be a place to stay and gives access to the river for fishing.

**River Mile 5**  Old Lake Ingram gives access to some of the river, a bit of Johnson Creek, and the lake itself. A canoe, boat, or tube would be required.

**River Mile 10**  There is a lake at Hays Park that can be reached via SH 16. Flotation is advised for the lake, but some river is available in the park for wade fishing.

**River Mile 14**  There is a small lake in Kerrville State Park. This area is stocked with rainbow trout during the winter by the state.

**River Mile 22**  This is the Lion's Park in Center Point, Texas. This area is very dirty. The water contains glass, bed springs, cans, etc. There might be pretty good sunfish fishing available if you want to try it. This is the only access between Kerrville and Center Point that can be used safely.

**River Mile 24**  This is the FM 1350 crossing about 2 miles southeast of Center Point. This is used by locals and is open above and below the crossing. There is easy parking and no posted signs.

**River Mile 41**  This is the second country road crossing off FM 473 east of Comfort, Texas, which is located in Kendall County. The road indicated is 3 miles east of I-10 and is a good site for a launch or wade fishing.

**River Mile 42.5**  This is a low-water crossing on a dirt road that turns right off the country road indicated at Mile 41. You could use this as a launch site to float to Waring, Texas, but there is some wade fishing available above and below the crossing as well.

**River Mile 44** This is a river crossing just north of Zoeller Lane in Waring, Texas. There is good access for wade fishing, but this would be an excellent launch for a float to Zoeller Crossing.

**River Mile 46** Follow Zoeller Lane east to Zoeller Crossing. This access is appropriate for wade fishing but is also a good launch site.

**River Mile 51** This is the FM 1376 crossing just south of Sisterdale, Texas. Some wade fishing is possible, but again it is a good take-out or launch site. The bass fishing between Zoeller Crossing and FM 1376 is very good.

**River Mile 61.5** This is the FM 474 crossing north of Boerne, Texas. Access can be achieved by going around the gate on the west side of the bridge. Good launch site for run to Bergheim Campground on FM 3351.

**River Mile 75.5** This is the Bergheim Campground and RV Park at the FM 3351 crossing of the river 5 miles north of Bergheim, Texas. They provide canoe rental, shuttle, fishing, and camping. There is also public access below the bridge. Call 210-336-2235. (Note that FM 3351 is a new number for this road — until 1993 it was designated FM 3160 and appears with that number on most maps.)

**River Mile 79.5** This is a crossing by Edge Falls Road that goes east off FM 3351 about 1 8/10 miles south of the Bergheim Campground. This would be a good take-out for a float from the campground or a launch site for a float to Guadalupe State Park.

**River Mile 83** This is Guadalupe State Park on SH 46 between Boerne and US 281. Camping is available, as well as fishing, but the park tends to be crowded.

**River Mile 87** In Comal County, there is a crossing 3 1/4 miles west of US 281 off SH 46. Take Spring Branch Road north to Spects Crossing. This is a potential launch site or take-out point. There is some fishing available by wading, but there is heavy use by locals and one would have to get far above or below the crossing to catch much.

**River Mile 90.5** This is Guadalupe Canoeing at US 281 and Guadalupe bridge south of Spring Branch, Texas. They provide canoe rental and shuttle service. Poor access to river otherwise.

**River Mile 92** This is the FM 311 crossing east of Spring Branch. Access is generally poor but can be gained by walking down from the northwest side of the bridge. There is some wade fishing available. Rebecca Creek Crossing has only poor access between Canyon Lake and FM 311 for white bass fishing in the spring. The best approach is to boat upstream into the river during the white bass run.

Here our interest turns to trout for at least 10 miles. Ed Engle's book *Fly Fishing the Tailwaters* gives a pretty good idea of what one will encounter on the Guadalupe River. Our dominant mayflies are the smaller species. The stoneflies are gone now. The caddis are prevalent, and there are good numbers of dragonflies and damselflies. The river has almost no scuds or sow bugs but does have good numbers of crayfish in red and green.

The two most prevalent mayflies are crawlers, the Paraleptophebia and Tricos. Trico nymphs occur in marl-rich bottoms. Paraleps occur in slow to medium water on leaves and twigs. We find Trico hatches are usually well handled by size #22-24 black spinners with crystal flash wings, since the molt from dun to spinner occurs almost immediately. One will occasionally have to use a small emerger, size #18, in olive or black. The Paraleps are well represented by Mahogany duns in size #18. A small Quill Gordon Nymph works great in the pre-hatch phase. Try a #16 to represent Paraleps emergers.

The next most common group is the swimmers, which include Baetis, Pseudocloeon, and Isonychia. The Isonychia Nymphs occur in the swifter parts of a stream and dart about like minnows. They are well represented by a Zug Bug. The duns hatch out of the water and are unavailable to the fish. The Pseudocloeon Nymphs occur in riffles and will occasionally cause a rise. The duns have olive bodies, grey wings, red eyes, and yellow legs and tails. A pretty little insect! They are about size #20. Baetis are found in underwater vegetation and will provoke a rise that is great fun to fish. A common place to find them is below the upper weir at the Kantz Lease and also just above the upper weir in the lake-like area. A Blue Winged Olive is the ticket in size #18.

The burrowers are represented by a Hexagenia species, probably *H. Carolina*, which is a huge insect. It is a yellowish brown with yellow wings. The duns are ignored for the most part. Try a twitch of the fly occasionally. This will often bring on a strike. Sometimes you will luck into a pre-hatch drift of emergers of these insects and the trout will porpoise for emergers. A chartreuse Woolly-worm works great. There seem to be fewer of these mayflies since the blow-out that occurred due to flooding in 1992 and 1993.

I suspect the burrower, Ephoron, is represented, since you will occasionally see a white mayfly on the water late in the evening. These are so few in number as to be insignificant.

The clingers are well represented, as there are three species of Stenomema present, the March Brown, Grey Fox, and Light Cahill. At least mayflies that are very similar to these eastern species are present. A Light Cahill for that insect and an Adams for the other two work very well. There is one Heptagenia species. Again it can be simulated satisfactorily by an Adams.

The best place to fish for trout in the Hill Country undoubtedly is the Guadalupe River below Canyon Dam, but several other streams are stocked or have been stocked in the past. These include the Blanco River in Blanco, Texas; the Llano River at Junction, Texas; the Pedernales River at LBJ State Park; and the South San Gabriel River at Georgetown, Texas. A list of waters stocked with trout in the winter can be obtained during the season from Texas Parks and Wildlife in Austin.

Here is a list of the flies we have found effective on the Guadalupe River. They should work equally well on the other streams mentioned.

*Dry Flies*
1. Adams #14 to #22
2. Light Cahill #14
3. Blue Winged Olive #18 to #20
4. Griffith's Gnat #16 to #20
5. Rusty Spinner #18
6. Trico Spinner #22 to #24
7. Black Ant #16 to #18
8. Brown Ant #18
9. Olive Spinner #18 to #20
10. Elk Hair Caddis #14
11. Mahogany Dun #18

*Nymphs*
1. Half-back #8 to #16
2. Woolly-worm in chartreuse #6
3. Gold Ribbed Hare's Ear #14 to #18
4. Pheasant Tail #14 to #16
5. Zug Bug #12 to #14
6. Girdle Bug #4 to #8
7. Picket Pin #12 to #14
8. Quill Gordon #16
9. Prince #12 to #14

*Wet Flies*
1. San Juan Worm #8
2. Quill Gordon #14 to #16
3. Black Gnat #12 to #14
4. Partridge and Green #14
5. Partridge and Orange #14

*Streamers or Deep-Running Flies*
1. Woolly-bugger in olive, black, olive and black #6
2. Clouser's Minnow #10
3. Clouser's Crayfish in olive
4. Joe's Mud Bug in olive or red

Most nymphs work well by casting down and across, allowing the nymph to rise to the surface, then working the nymph upstream with a slow strip retrieve. Most strikes occur as the nymph begins to rise at the end of the swing. This technique works well for wet flies as well.

The subtle twitch of a dry fly on the surface seems to induce strikes occasionally. This is particularly true with caddis patterns such as the elk hair caddis. Try to make the caddis jump upstream.

These fish, even though they are stocked fish, can become selective, so try to match your dry flies to the hatching duns. If you are not successful with dries, try emerger patterns. You can use a nymph if you do not have emergers with you. Put fly floatant on the leader and tippet down to within 2 or 3 inches of the fly. This will suspend the nymph just under the surface film. You must match the size of the dun pretty closely, but you can get away with one or two hook sizes larger most of the time.

The number of hatching Grey Fox and March Browns is sharply reduced since the floods of '92 and '93. If and when these mayflies return in significant numbers, the use of the artificials representing the Grey Fox or March Brown may become more important.

To check the release by the Army Corps of Engineers into the river below Canyon Dam, call 210-964-3342. A release of 600 cfs or more is dangerous for wading. About 300 cfs or less is ideal. The recording you will hear is updated daily, but the flow can be changed at any time during the day. (This is not in itself that dangerous, since the rise of the river is generally slow and steady.) The biggest inconvenience for the fly-fisher on this stretch of the Guadalupe is recreational tubers. During weekends in the spring and fall, and every day during the summer, the rubber hatch is on from mid-morning till sundown.

**River Mile 116** Corps of Engineers Park below the dam. There is good access to the river for about 1/2 mile below the dam. The area is frequently crowded with bait fishermen. There is the potential for stripers on streamers, but most of the fishing is for stocked rainbows. This is a good launch site, but you would have to portage down a steep hill from the parking lot.

**River Mile 118.5** This is a bridge on FM 306 about 2 miles east of Canyon City. Access is very poor. The Maricopa Ranch Resort sits west of the bridge and has access to the river and is a good place to stay. Their number is 210-964-3600. They also have a RV park (210-964-3731).

**River Mile 119.5** This is a second crossing by FM 306. This is just beyond the junction of FM 306 and FM 2673. There is a private camp that gives access for a fee. They also rent canoes. One can park on the road shoulder and enter the river under the bridge for wade fishing downstream for a short distance. There are two weirs in the stretch of water below this area, containing Trout Unlimited's Kantz Lease. It is not advisable to trespass in this area. If you would like information about membership in Trout Unlimited, the address of the national organization is P.O. Box 1335, Merrifield, VA 22116. There is a toll-free number for membership services: 800-834-2419. There are two chapters in Texas; the leases on the Guadalupe are managed by the Guadalupe River Chapter, which can be contacted through membership personnel in Austin (Alan Bray, 512-263-9619), Houston (Judy Presswood, 713-932-7874), and San Antonio (Jon Morse, 210-493-7132). The Brazos Chapter, covering North Texas, can be contacted through David Hurdle, P.O. Box 1201, Azle, TX 76098.

**River Mile 121** This is a bridge crossing on River Road east of Sattler. A private camp gives access for a fee for parking or wade fishing above the bridge. Good launch site for float through one of the more popular areas of the river.

**River Mile 122.5** This is Ponderosa Bridge access, which is under control of TU. You must be a member with a lease card to access this area.

**River Mile 123** L and L Campground. This is under control of TU during the winter months but would be available for access during the summer for bass and sunfish. There is the potential for a holdover trout as well.

**River Mile 125** This is Beans Camp, about 5 miles down River Road. This area is heavily stocked by the state with 6- to 8-inch rainbows. The fishing can be quite good. Overnight camping is permitted, and there are toilet facilities and picnic tables available.

**River Mile 128** There is poor access at this crossing. Use the several private camps along the river for access to smallmouth and sunfish fishing.

**River Mile 130** This is Hueco Springs. Can be used for float to Gruene, Texas. This float covers large smallmouth and some huge sunfish. This is best attempted in the fall after the tubers are gone from the river. There is some limited wade fishing at Hueco Springs.

**River Mile 133** This is Gruene, Texas. There is some good sunfish fishing by floating through several park areas in New Braunfels. The bass fishing is generally poor.

A number of accommodations offering access to the river all along its course have been mentioned already. Beginning at the main stem of the Guadalupe in Hunt, some other possibilities should be mentioned.

Hunt has a small store for soft drinks, beer, and some food supplies. Access is poor in Hunt. Try the Casa Del Rio Cottages for access and information. Their number is 210-238-4424.

The Hunter House Motel in Ingram would be a nice place to stay and use as a jumping-off place to go up or down the river.

In Kerrville, The Inn of The Hills River Resort at 210-895-5000 is a very nice place to stay and is moderately priced. There is a good restaurant on the premises. The Kerrville Bed and Breakfast at 210-257-8750 and the La Reata Ranch Bed and Breakfast at 210-896-5503 are available if you wish to go that route.

Kerrville has several fine restaurants that we can recommend. These include the Cowboy Steak House, Acapulco Restaurant, Mamacita's, Mencius Gourmet Hunan, and the Sunday House Inn Restaurant. The latter is excellent but a little expensive.

Boerne, Texas, has several nice restaurants including Saliano's Italian Restaurant, Country Spirit Restaurant, and the Cowboy Steak House. The Po Po Family Restaurant at Welfare, Texas, also has an excellent reputation. Motels that are very adequate include The Key to the Hills, 800-690-5763, and the Texas Country Inn at 210-249-9791. One would have to contact the Chamber of Commerce for a list of bed and breakfasts, if any exist.

There are good restaurants in Gruene and New Braunfels. One of our favorites is the Clear Springs Restaurant on SH 46 toward Seguin. The better motels include the Hill Country Motor Inn, 800-982-3609, and the Roadway Inn, 800-967-1168. The Danville School and Historic Kuebler-Waldrip Haus Bed and Breakfast at 800-299-8372 is the only one with which we are familiar.

Camping is available on Canyon Lake at multiple sites through the Army Corps of Engineers by calling 210-964-3341. These sites include Canyon Park, Cranes Mill Park, Potters Creek Park, Jacobs Creek Park, North Park, and Comal Park.

In Gruene you might want to drop in to visit Ray Box at Gruene Outfitters (1629 Hunter Road, 210-625-4440). The shop is open every day except Christmas and Thanksgiving and offers fly-fishing gear, river gear, books, maps, etc. They also book fly-fishing trips in the Hill Country (and elsewhere), and offer casting instruction daily.

# Lampasas River

FOUND ON PAGES 101 AND 102 OF THE ROADS OF TEXAS

This is a pretty stream that runs through Hamilton, Lampasas, Burnet, and Bell counties. There is no access in Hamilton County.

**River Mile 0** CR 105 in Lampasas County goes west off US 281 about 22 miles north of Lampasas, Texas. Cross the bridge and enter on the southwest side.

**River Mile 6** This is the US 281 crossing about 15 miles north of Lampasas. The best access is on the southwest side of the bridge. The water is clear, but the flow is low.

**River Mile 12** This is the crossing of RR 1690, which goes east off US 281 about 13 miles northeast of Lampasas. This is posted on the south side, but access is good on the north. There are large numbers of bass to two pounds and good numbers of sunfish of average size.

**River Mile 18** This is the RR 580 crossing about 10 miles northeast of Lampasas at Rumley. There is considerable local use. Good holes are found above and below the crossing.

**River Mile 22** This is the RR 2313 crossing about 5 miles north of Kempner, Texas. There is good access, but some posted signs are present, so be careful. RR 2313 leaves RR 580 4 miles south of Rumley and crosses the river en route to Kempner.

**River Mile 26** This is the US 190 crossing 1 mile west of Kempner. There is no access due to fencing and posted signs. A county road that crosses the river just above this crossing is also posted and no longer available.

**River Mile 40.5** In Burnet County, FM 2657 crosses about 1 mile north of Okalla, Texas. You would need to be a goat to access the river from the south or lower end of the bridge. The upper end is posted very emphatically.

**River Mile 48.5** Burnet CR 220 leaves FM 2657 south of Okalla and crosses over into Bell County. It crosses the river at a tall bridge just to the right at Maxdale community (this is the second high bridge you will cross—the first is over a large creek). Access is at the southeast corner of the bridge. There are no signs, and the area is obviously used by the locals. There is plenty of potential for wade fishing above and below the crossing in several good holes.

**River Mile 79** The only other worthwhile access in Bell County is the Chalk Ridge Falls Park below Stillhouse Hollow Dam. Walk downstream from the lake outlet to the end of the nature trails for good wade fishing. The water is clear. Below this area at the I-35 crossing the river is muddy and gets progressively more muddy. The other access points above the reservoir are fenced and posted.

In Lampasas, the motels that look good include the Circle Motel, 800-521-5417 or local call 556-6201, and the Saratoga Motel at 512-556-6244. The Moses Hughes Ranch is the only listed bed and breakfast. Call 512-556-5923. They do not take children and do not allow smoking. A list of restaurants should include The Courtyard Cafe, Liverman's Ranch House Bar-B-Q, Pizza Hut, and the China Inn.

In Salado, Texas, the Ho-Jo Motel at 817-947-5000 is quite nice. The Stagecoach Inn is famous, but I suspect somewhat expensive. Their number is 817-947-5111.

For camping in the area, try the KOA Campground in Belton, Texas. Motels in the Belton area include the Roadway Inn at 817-939-0744, the Ramada Inn at 817-939-3745, and the River Forest Motel at 817-939-5711.

# Llano River

FOUND ON PAGES 115 AND 116 OF THE ROADS OF TEXAS

The south and north forks of the Llano join in Junction, Texas. The north fork has more of the character of the main stem of the river, but access is poor. There is a Camp Allison, which gives access off I-10, northwest of Roosevelt, Texas. Take the road to the right at the yellow windmill and go south. This is a good place to take the family for a picnic. For the best fishing, you would need a boat or tube. This is located in Sutton County.

The south fork arises in northern Edwards County and is a beautiful, clear stream. It is lined by deciduous trees and remains cooler than the main river. Wade fishing is possible, but the best approach is to float between the various access points. The Llano offers the best chance to catch a largemouth bass of eight or more pounds of all the Texas Hill Country streams. The average size of the Guadalupe bass is larger on this stream as well. The dominant sunfish in this stream is the yellowbelly, but some large bluegills are present. Occasionally, green perch will be caught, but long ears, red ears, Rio Grande perch, and rock bass are rare or nonexistent.

**River Mile 0** This is a low-water crossing 11 miles southwest of Junction on US 377. I have seen largemouth of five or more pounds above this crossing, and the fishing for Guadalupe bass is very good.

**River Mile 9.75** This is the entrance to the Buck's Wildlife Management Area southwest of Junction on US 377. This is about 9 miles below the previous crossing by river. Camping is available. I have seen largemouth in excess of six pounds in the large hole above the crossing into the management area. The area below is wadeable but is hit pretty hard. A float from the previous crossing to the management area would be ideal.

**River Mile 15.25** City Park and I-10 bridge in Junction. This area will produce good bass and sunfish fishing below the dam. Weighted nymphs should work quite well for large sunfish and some bass in the lake area.

**River Mile 37.25** RR 385 crossing Llano River off US 377 between Junction and London, Texas. Use a flotation device above the river crossing. The area below is wadeable for sunfish and some bass fishing. The Texas Fly Fishers from Houston have floated between Junction and RR 385 several times for excellent catches of bass and sunfish. This requires at least one overnight camp-out since this float covers 22 river miles.

**River Mile 59.25** In Mason County, FM 1871 crosses the river west of Mason, Texas. This is a potential take-out from the previous crossing of RR 385 but is about 22 miles of floating and would require a camp-out. There is a large hole below that is very good in the upper end for Guadalupe bass. This is a good launch site for a float downstream of some 4 1/2 miles. The fishing is quite good.

**River Mile 63.75** This is the FM 2389 crossing south of Mason. FM 2389 is a branch off FM 1723, which goes south out of Mason opposite the city park. There is a large island above the crossing that permits day use and camping. Fishing above the island is quite good for large sunfish and bass of all four species.

**River Mile 69.75** Crossing of FM 1723 south of Mason. There have been one seven- and two six-pound largemouths caught here during the last year. Good take-out from the FM 2389 crossing, which is a float of about 6 miles. This allows fishing over some large bass and sunfish.

**River Mile 73.75** The US 87 crossing of the Llano south of Hedwig's Hill. Access is southeast of the bridge. There is a very large hole below the crossing that would make flotation mandatory for best fishing. The area above the crossing is wadeable, but the river is split in multiple channels, and wading would be potentially hazardous. The same can be said for a float from above due to maneuvering between the rocks. Almost constant portage is required for the last 1/2 mile of this float, but the fishing is said to be very good.

**River Mile 82** In Llano County, FM 2768 crosses the river after leaving RR 152 in Castell, Texas. There is fair fishing for Guadalupe bass above the crossing and for sunfish and Guadalupe bass below the crossing. The 8-mile float from Hedwig's Hill is said to be very good.

**River Mile 86.5** This is the CR 103 crossing 4 1/2 miles east of Castell. CR 103 is off RR 152. This crossing is about 4 1/2 miles below the previous crossing at Castell. The river here is very fine for medium-sized bass and some large sunfish.

**River Mile 91** Scott Crossing on CR 102 9 miles east of Castell and 8 1/2 miles west of Llano, Texas, off RR 152. Very good bass and large sunfish above and below the crossing.

The entire area between Castell and Scott Crossing is a potential area for floating. One could make a float of 9 miles or two floats of 4 1/2 miles each. The latter would be our personal choice because of more time to fish the best areas.

**River Mile 99** This is the city lake in Llano, Texas. This gives good access for boat or float tube fishing in the lake. The bass and sunfish fishing should be quite good, especially in the spring and fall with surface lures.

**River Mile 100.75** This is the Highway 16 bridge crossing in Llano. The best access is on the southeast side of the crossing. Good potential for Guadalupe bass and sunfish in the multiple channels of the river.

The Goodman Ranch offers cabins for lease on the south fork. These are nice people. One of their cabins will sleep eight people. The telephone number is 915-446-3870; their address is Rt. HC 15, Box 251, Junction, Texas 76849. Camping is available at the South Llano River State Park, 915-446-3994, and in Junction, at KOA Campground, 915-446-3138.

In the Junction area, the Best Western River Valley Inn at Segovia, 915-446-3331, and in Junction, the Day's Inn, 915-446-3730, and the Carousel Inn, 915-446-3301, are good motels. Try Isacks Restaurant and La Familia Mexican Restaurant for food in Junction. Isacks has good country food, and La Familia has great Mexican food.

In Mason, Texas, the Hill Country Inn, 915-347-6317, is a nice motel. Try the Chamber of Commerce for a list of bed and breakfasts. The Zavala Mexican Restaurant and Cooper's Bar-B-Q are both quite good. Cooper's is famous far and wide — Zavala's is very good for breakfast. Camping is available at Fort Mason City Park. The number is 915-347-6656.

Two of the bed-and-breakfast establishments available in Llano, Texas, are the Badu House, 915-247-4304, and the Fraser Haus Inn, 915-247-5183. Camping is available at the Llano County Community Center, 915-247-5354, and Robinson City Park, 915-247-4158. Cooper's Bar-B-Q is available in Llano as well as Mason and is just as good. There are other good restaurants available and include Meme's Family Restaurant, Inmann Restaurant, and the Chaparral Hungry Hunter. The Chaparral Motor Inn in Llano, 915-247-4111, is adequate for men but is old. The ladies would probably enjoy the newer Classic Inn more.

# Medina River

FOUND ON PAGE 128 OF THE ROADS OF TEXAS

Our area of interest on the Medina River is confined to Bandera County and is relatively short. The river below Medina Lake has poor access except for a private camp just below the dam.

The Medina is readily available from San Antonio, the upper reaches of the north prong being only 65 miles from Loop 410. The west prong has no access, which is unfortunate since this is a good-looking stream with some good-sized bass. Some of the access points have been lost recently due to new construction of roads and the placement of fences and posted signs. This river is still worth a look.

There are some large bass in the more remote areas on the Medina, and the sunfish species are varied and large on the average. The only one missing is the Rio Grande perch. Streamers work very well on bass, and the sunfish respond to streamers better on this river than on any other Hill Country stream. My favorite lures remain the various small hair bugs and poppers, however.

**River Mile 0**  This is the farthest crossing of the north fork of the river by FR 2107. FR 2107 goes west off SH 16 about 3 4/10 miles north of Medina, Texas. This large pool is used by the locals for swimming and is deep. Wade fishing is almost impossible above or below. You can get about much better with a tube or canoe in the upper pool. There are some small bass and sunfish to be caught. Not recommended as a launch site due to problems of trespass and shallow, rough water below.

**River Mile 1.5**  This is the middle crossing of FM 2107. Poor access generally, but there is some wade fishing available downstream. Again, this portion of the stream is not floatable and is subject to trespass problems due to development along the banks.

**River Mile 3.25**  This is known as Rocky Creek Crossing. There is good access to a large pool above the crossing, which contains some large bass at times. Sunfish are prevalent here as well. The area downstream is now posted, but the plunge pool just below the crossing is available and frequently has some bass and an occasional large sunfish. It is possible to float from here to the next access, but it is a rough trip and not recommended. This area does contain large numbers of good-sized bass and sunfish. This float covers about 3 to 4 river miles but seems much longer due to frequent portages and drags.

**River Mile 6.25**  This is the SH 16 crossing about 4 4/10 miles north of Medina, Texas. Use this as a take-out only. The area above is posted, and there have been problems with landowners below. Go to the Baxter Ranch just south of the crossing on the left and gain access for a small fee. These are nice people. You will need a canoe or tube to do the area justice.

**River Mile 10** Some fly-fishers enter the river west of Medina where RR 337 crosses the river on its way to Vanderpool. We believe there is the potential for problems here and recommend you enter the river at Moffett Park 1 mile downstream. Turn west toward the river on Patterson Street and cross the small bridge. Parking is available immediately to the right after you cross the river. Walk up- or downstream from here. This is a good launch site for a float downstream and is the first launch site recommended by Fred Collins, who operates a rental and shuttle service in Bandera. Call Fred at 210-796-3553.

**River Mile 13** This is a low-water bridge on a country road about 1 3/4 miles south of Medina. This is a take-out point only; do not leave your car parked here, as this is a private crossing. There have been some large bass (four to five pounds) between Medina and this take-out point.

**River Mile 14** This is a crossing under SH 16 about 2 3/4 miles southeast of Medina. This is a potential take-out point only.

**River Mile 19.5** Peaceful Valley Ranch Road gives poor access due to a new bridge and fencing. Use with caution as a take-out or launch site due to narrow road and bridge.

**River Mile 23** SH 16 crosses the river 3 miles west of Bandera, Texas. Easy access for occasional large sunfish and small bass. Tables are available in the small roadside park. There is a large pool below for tube or canoe. Good launch site for float downstream to the next crossing.

**River Mile 24** This is the FR 470 crossing on the road to Tarpley, Texas. You gain good access to the river below here. The next bridge, about 1/2 mile below 470, is private, and the owners do not want the crossing used. About 3 miles down from 470 you will come upon the Bandera Beverage Barn, which has mowed river access, food and refreshments, and is a good, safe take-out point. The area immediately below here is somewhat dangerous, and Fred Collins, who has extensive experience on this river, does not recommend floating below the Beverage Barn. Bandera City Park is about 5 miles below this access.

**River Mile 28** Bandera City Park affords good access, but the fish are small. This is a good launch site for a float to Bandera Falls about 10 miles downstream. Fred Collins points out that this is one of the areas where you don't want to lose a canoe or be injured due to the remoteness of the area.

**River Mile 39** This is the Ruede Ranch. The ranch can be reached by going southeast toward Medina Lake on FM 1283 at Pipe Creek, Texas. Cross the bridge over Red Bluff Creek and turn right on the first dirt road just before the crest of the hill. Take the left when you come to a fork in the road. Take another left and follow the signs that say "to the river." Stop at the house and pay a small fee, and you will be directed to the parking area. You must cross some suspension bridges to get to the river. Cross the river and fish up- or downstream. There are some good-sized bass and large sunfish, primarily bluegills and yellow-belly perch, up and down the river. There is the potential for white bass fishing in the spring since this is just above Medina Lake.

## Food & Lodging on the Medina

In Bandera, the Bandera Lodge at 210-796-3093 is a good place to stay. There is a new motel, the River Oaks Motel and Restaurant (210-796-7751), and there is also the River Front Motel (210-460-3690), which is said to have the best accommodations.

Bed-and-breakfast establishments include Bandera Creek, 210-796-3517, Diamond H Ranch, 210-796-4820, and Hill Country Island off SH 46, 210-535-4050.

Camping is available at the Hill Country State Natural Area, 210-796-4413, at Bandera County Park, which is known as Mansfield Park (210-796-3168) 1/2 mile below the FM 470 crossing on SH 16, and at the Bandera Beverage Barn (210-796-8153).

The Pipe Creek Junction Cafe in Pipe Creek, and Harvey's Old Bank Steak House and Serranos Cafe in Bandera are recommended.

# Nueces River

FOUND ON PAGE 127 OF THE ROADS OF TEXAS

The Nueces River begins above Vance, Texas, but is intermittent in flow until it arrives south of Vance. Access for fishing in the area above Vance is poor and not recommended.

The preponderance of fish in the area around Vance are native largemouth bass and bluegill sunfish. As one moves downstream, the dominance of the largemouths decreases due to heavy stocking of Guadalupe bass by the state, and the variety of the sunfish changes. The numbers of yellow-belly sunfish, rock bass, green perch, and Rio Grande perch increase significantly, though the bluegills remain the dominant species.

The upper river is crystal clear and in beautiful surroundings. Trash on the banks becomes a problem just north and west of Uvalde due to use of access points by locals. Trash is also a problem at the Barksdale crossing. One can overcome this problem by getting about 1/2 mile above or below the crossings (and by carrying out some trash yourself!). Several areas are floatable, especially between Lake Nueces and the crossing by US 83 north of La Pryor, Texas.

Use light tackle and have a ball. It would not be unusual for an experienced fly-fisher to catch fifty to one hundred fish in a day of fishing on this river. There is the potential of catching a very big largemouth bass here as well.


**River Mile 0** This access sits on the line between Real and Edwards counties. This is about 1/4 mile below Vance, Texas. There are lots of small largemouth and good-sized bluegills. Walk upriver if not fenced about 3/4 of a mile to a large pool. There is occasionally very good fishing around some downed trees. Downstream there is a run that will usually give up several bass to one pound. Fish every small hole under bushes, etc., to get to all the areas that will likely hold fish.

**River Mile 7** Take the only road to the east in Barksdale, Texas, to the river crossing. This is off SH 55. The large hole above would require a boat or float tube to adequately fish. The area below the crossing is wadeable. The water is very clear. One can see freshwater shrimp swimming in the water near the bank. Lost Canyon Campground is 4 miles down this road, located on Dry Creek. Cabins are available that will sleep up to ten people, and there is excellent fishing for bass and sunfish in the 10-acre pond on the grounds. The phone number is 512-348-3222, which is the owner's office, not located at the campground. When the owner is away, Perry and Kathy Hicks (210-234-3133) at the Fina station in Barksdale handle rentals.

**River Mile 10** SH 55 crossing south of Barksdale. There is a big hole above the crossing. Some parts are wadeable, but it would be best to use some flotation for best fishing.

**River Mile 14** This is off SH 55 in Camp Wood, Texas. Turn west 1 block north of the city park on an unpaved road that leads to the river. There are several areas along this road that lend themselves to good access. This is close to town so is hard hit. There are some big bluegills and an occasional good-sized largemouth. One can occasionally get into Rio Grande perch on poppers. This is a good take-out point or launch site for floats.

**River Mile 19.5** This is the SH 55 crossing at Lake Nueces about 4 miles below Camp Wood. The lake has some large bass in the upper end and is very good for large sunfish on poppers. One would need a boat or float tube. South of the crossing, there is a large pool with many Guadalupe bass. However, this pool has suffered recently from the building of the new bridge over the river. You could launch here for a float to the next access and get into some excellent fishing, but it is rough going.

**River Mile 25.5** Witt Crossing is in Uvalde County. This is a dirt road that goes east off SH 55 and gives access to the river. Will periodically have good sunfish and largemouth bass fishing. Good take-out or launch site.

**River Mile 27.5** CR 412 gives access to the river at Montell, Texas. Very good sunfish to a half pound. These are generally yellow-bellies or bluegills. There will occasionally be large bass, but the river is generally loaded with Guadalupe bass to ten inches. Flotation is necessary for the area above the crossing. This is a good launch site.

**River Mile 30** This is the CR 410 crossing south of Montell off SH 55. Cross the river to park. Excellent sunfish to half a pound and occasional largemouth to three pounds but mostly Guadalupe bass. Fish above and below the crossing. Use polaroids and site cast to Guadalupe bass in the small pools. This is a good launch site.

**River Mile 33** This is the CR 408 crossing off SH 55. Cross the river and park on the east side. This area has excellent sunfish and bass fishing above and below the crossing. This would be a good launch site for a float to 19-mile crossing, which is about 6 1/2 miles below by river. You would see some pretty water and have an easy float.

**River Mile 39.5** This is the crossing of SH 55 about 19 miles north of Uvalde, Texas. This access gets heavy day use by locals. Fish the east bank above for small bass and sunfish. There is fair fishing below the crossing if you are willing to walk.

**River Mile 41.5** Camp Chalk Bluff. Camping and cabins are available. Some fishing is available in large pools. This is a potential launch site if water flow is adequate. In extended dry spells the river tends to run under the gravel.

**River Mile 43.5** Take CR 405 west to the river. This access receives heavy use by locals, and there is considerable trash. There are large holes above and below the crossing that contain some small bass and lots of sunfish.

**River Mile 58** This is the US 90 crossing west of Uvalde. Good launch site for float. There is good potential for bass and sunfish catches above and below the crossing about 1/4 mile.

**River Mile 66.5** This is the FM 481 crossing of the Nueces 8 miles southwest of Uvalde. This road is known as the Old Eagle Pass Road. This crossing is heavily used by locals but has some fishing for small bass and sunfish above and below the crossing. This is a good launch site for a float to the US 83 crossing south of Uvalde if there is adequate flow.

**River Mile 75** In Zavala County, US 83 crosses the river southwest of Uvalde and creates a good access point. There is heavy use by locals, and a lot of trash has accumulated. The best fishing is 1 mile below the crossing. There are largemouth to three pounds and very good warmouth, or rock bass, fishing against the banks. Good bluegill fishing occurs in this same area for 2 miles below the crossing. If you have four-wheel drive, you can drive to the best fishing.

**River Mile 88** This is a potential take-out point for a float from the previous crossing but encompasses about 13 river miles. This access is created by the crossing of US 57 east of La Pryor, Texas.

**River Mile 111** This is Upper Nueces Lake, which has good sunfish fishing but is rather poor for bass. In the spring, there is a great Hexagenia hatch in the twilight and at night. Take FM 1025 off US 83 to the campground and the boat ramp.

## Food & Lodging on the Nueces

The Old Timer Cafe in Camp Wood provides adequate meals at a reasonable cost. There is also a very good Mexican food restaurant in Camp Wood. Camping is available at Lake Nueces Park 4 miles south of Camp Wood. Call 210-597-3223.

In Uvalde, the Vasquez Cafe has excellent food. Haby's Bar-B-Q is quite good. The Amber Sky Motel has a very good restaurant. The pastries are especially enjoyable. There is a bed-and-breakfast establishment called Casa De Leona in Uvalde. Call 210-278-8550 for reservations. The Continental Inn, 210-278-5671; the Holiday Inn, 210-278-4511; and The Inn of Uvalde, 210-278-9173, are all nice motels.

# Pedernales River

FOUND ON PAGES 117 AND 118 OF THE ROADS OF TEXAS

The Pedernales River is a small stream that arises east of Harper, Texas, in Gillespie County and flows almost due east. This river is unusual in that it begins somewhat murky and clears as it flows through Blanco County toward its union with the Colorado River. The Pedernales is loaded with carp, thanks to our German ancestors, who stocked this and other rivers with them. These fish can weigh forty or more pounds, and they create a problem when they begin to spawn by creating silt that covers other fish nests. There is some good fishing available on this stream, but it must be searched for, as it is not as readily available as on other streams.

**River Mile 0** In Gillespie County, the first possible access is on Fielder Road, east of Harper. This road branches off FM 2093 about 5 7/10 miles east of Harper. The stream is quite small here and would require permission. We do not know if the property owner will grant permission to fish. Be sure to ask!

**River Mile 2** This is Friedrich Road Crossing off FM 2093, which is 6 7/10 miles east of Harper. The area above the crossing is fenced, but there is a beautiful hole below that would require flotation to do it justice. Again, we recommend that you seek permission but do not know if it would be granted.

**River Mile 6.5** This is White Oak Road Crossing, which is not recommended due to fencing and logistic problems.

**River Mile 11** This is the Morris-Tivy Dale Road, about 16 miles east of Harper off FM 2093. There is some use by locals. There are no posted signs or fences. There is good potential both directions from the crossing. This would be a good launch site for a float through the SH 16 crossing southwest of Fredericksburg to Pfeister Road, since the SH 16 crossing is fenced and it would not be possible to take out there.

**River Mile 15** This is Pfeister Road, 2 river miles downstream from the SH 16 crossing. This road leaves SH 16 to the southeast about 2 miles from the SH 16 bridge.

**River Mile 15.75** This is Center Point Road off SH 16 southwest of Fredericksburg, Texas. You should float this stretch due to posted signs. This road joins River Road, which follows the river east to US 87.

**River Mile 19.5** This is Old Kerrville Road that intersects River Road after Old Kerrville Road leaves SH 16. This is a good access for wade fishing but could best be fished below with a tube or canoe. Good launch site for float to US 87 crossing. This is about 2 river miles.

**River Mile 21.5** This is the US 87 crossing of the river south of Fredericksburg. There is good access along the River Road for short distances. Should be good for small bass and sunfish. There are multiple road crossings east of Fredericksburg off US 290 that are not recommended due to shallowness, posting, or fencing of the river, etc.

**River Mile 39** For the next 5 miles of the river there are multiple sites for access on RR 1 in LBJ State Park and the National Park. This area is stocked with rainbow trout periodically during the winter. The water is very clear. There are multiple dams, and some type of water craft is recommended for the best fishing opportunity.

**River Mile 49** This is the FM 1320 crossing north of US 290. This is a good access, and wade fishing is possible, but the water is shallow at the crossing.

**River Mile 62** This is a small lake created by a dam on the river in Johnson City. Some type of flotation is necessary. Access can be gained on the southwest side of the crossing of US 281 north of Johnson City.

**River Mile 78** This is Pedernales Falls State Park. This is a beautiful setting and gives good access for small bass and sunfish. The pools are loaded with large carp. This may be a launch site for a downstream float, but permission must be granted by the Park Rangers. One would launch from the swimming area.

**River Mile 93** This is Hammett's Crossing on a dirt road off SH 71 in Travis County. Ask directions as this is very difficult to find. This is about 15 miles below the park by the river.

**River Mile 99** This is the SH 71 crossing of the river, which gives very poor access. There is a private camp for access just below the crossing.

The Milton Reimer's ranch gives good access for white bass fishing. Take the Hamilton Pool Road left off SH 71 about 2 miles past Bee Caves. The ranch entrance is about 13 miles from the intersection. Go to the ranch house for instructions.

## Food & Lodging on the Pedernales

There are several excellent restaurants available in Fredericksburg. We can recommend Friedhelm's Bavarian Inn and Bar, George's Old German Bakery and Restaurant, and the Altdorf Biergarten.

Camping is available at the Lady Bird Johnson Municipal Park south of Fredericksburg. The number is 210-997-4202.

A list of good motels should include the Save Inn, 210-997-6568; the

Comfort Inn, 800-424-6423; and the Sunday House Motel, 210-997-4484. The Econolodge is also quite nice.

Bed and Breakfasts of Fredericksburg has twenty-five locations. The number is 210-997-4712. Be My Guest has thirty-five locations. The number is 210-997-7227.

The two places in Johnson City for food are Pasquales Mexican Food and the Charles Restaurant. Camping is available at Pedernales Falls State Park. Call 210-868-7304. Numerous bed-and-breakfast establishments can be contacted via the Chamber of Commerce at 210-868-7684. The Save Inn Motel, 210-868-4044, and the Charles Motel, 210-868-7171, are both nice motels in Johnson City.

# Sabinal River

FOUND ON PAGE 127 OF THE ROADS OF TEXAS

The Sabinal River is a small river arising in the western portion of Bandera County. It flows south into Uvalde County, where it goes underground. This is a very scenic river that contains some large bass in the more remote areas. These areas are somewhat difficult to get to and are best reached by canoe.

**River Mile 0** Lost Maples State Natural Area is the first access area on the Sabinal. The upper reaches of the river are quite shallow, but the natural area contains some very good fishing for average-sized Guadalupe bass and small sunfish, predominately bluegills, that are very colorful. The bass are found in small holes above and below a small lake on upper Can Creek and in the Sabinal River below its confluence with the creek.

**River Mile 7** This is the crossing of the river by RR 187 about 1 1/2 miles below the junction of RR 337 and RR 187. The river above is fenced, but there is access below to small bass and sunfish.

**River Mile 11** The next crossing by RR 187 gets heavy local use for swimming. There are posted signs below, but there is a very large pool above that is quite deep and requires some type of flotation to be adequately fished. There are occasional catches of large bass here, and there will always be large perch available.

**River Mile 15** This is the RR 1050 crossing off RR 187 in Utopia. The river is dammed here, and the resultant small lake can be fished with a float tube or canoe. The plunge pool and river below the dam contain some nice largemouth and good-sized sunfish that can be reached by wade fishing.

**River Mile 19** This is a crossing by RR 187 south of Utopia. Access is very poor because of posted signs and fences. The best approach would be to stay at Utopia on The River, a bed-and-breakfast establishment that is just above this crossing, and fish their waters. One could use this access for a launch to the next crossing some 5 miles by river. This is a rough trip, but you would float over some good bass and sunfish.

**River Mile 24** This is the second RR 187 crossing south of Utopia. There is fencing across the river below, but there is fair to good fishing above if you will walk up about 1/4 mile.

**River Mile 42** The US 90 crossing west of Sabinal, Texas, will occasionally contain good bass and sunfish. The river goes under the gravel above this but comes up and creates some nice water below the bridge and downstream. There are two low-water crossings off RR 187 south of Sabinal that may give access. One would need to inquire in town, since they are difficult to locate and may be blocked off. The first is said to be 3 miles south, the second is 4 miles south. Worth a look.

**River Mile 53** This is the RR 187 crossing about 15 miles south of Sabinal. There is a large pool above the crossing and some good water below the crossing for several hundred yards.

## Food & Lodging on the Sabinal

Camping is available at Lost Maples. The number is 210-966-3413. Bed-and-breakfast establishments include Utopia on the River, south of Utopia, Texas, and Tubb's Heritage House at Vanderpool, Texas. Fox-fire Cabins in Vanderpool (210-966-2200) offers nice accommodations directly on the river.

The Lost Maples Cafe in Utopia is quite good for country cooking at reasonable prices.

# San Gabriel River

FOUND ON PAGES 102 AND 117 OF THE ROADS OF TEXAS

The San Gabriel River has a north and south fork that join in Georgetown, Texas. I will indicate potential access points on each fork, as well as the main stem. The upper reaches of both forks tend to be shallow and are somewhat difficult to gain access to. There are good numbers of fish, especially on the north fork and the main river.

## South Fork

**River Mile 0** In Burnet County, there is only one access. This is off FM 1174 south of Bertram, Texas. Take CR 322 for about 1 mile, then turn right on CR 323. Use a canoe above and wade below.

**River Mile 8** In Williamson County, FM 1869 crosses the river southwest of Liberty Hill. Lots of trash. Walk up- and downstream to get to the best fishing. Go at least 1/4 mile.

**River Mile 19** This is the US 183 crossing southeast of Liberty Hill. Access is open to upstream or downstream wade fishing. Good numbers of bass in the holes.

**River Mile 20** This is the CR 270 crossing. CR 270 goes east off US 183 just south of the US 183 crossing at Mile 19. This is a low-water crossing. The best fishing is below the crossing.

**River Mile 22** CR 268 off SH 29 crosses the river southeast of Liberty Hill. Another approach would be to take FM 2243 to the east of Leander, Texas, and turn north on CR 268. Go below for the best fishing.

**River Mile 30** This is the I-35 crossing in Georgetown. This part of the stream is available, but it is doubtful if it is very worthwhile due to its proximity to town.

## North Fork

**River Mile 0** In Burnet County, there is a crossing with access at Joppa, Texas, northeast of Bertram, Texas. Take FM 243 northeast from Bertram and turn left on CR 272. You will cross the Russell Fork of the San Gabriel in about 4 miles. Continue for about 1 mile to the intersection with CR 200. Turn right to the access and parking on the southeast side of the bridge. Good fishing in pool above and below bridge.

**River Mile 16** In Williamson County, there is a crossing reached by taking CR 207 off US 183 to the left. Turn left on the first paved road about 2 1/2 miles off US 183. The river is fenced below, but the upstream area is open. The river is shallow.

**River Mile 20** This is the US 183 crossing northeast of Liberty Hill. A road leads to the river from the southeast side of the bridge. There is good wade fishing above and below the crossing.

**River Mile 21** This is the river crossing of CR 257. Take FM 3405 to the east off US 183. Turn south on CR 257. There are no fences or signs. There is easy wade fishing in both directions.

**River Mile 24** This is the CR 258 crossing. Take FM 3405 off US 183 or off FM 2338 out of Georgetown. Turn south on CR 258 to the crossing. Good access to the river. This is a good area in the spring for white bass that run up from Lake Georgetown. The Tejas Camp is located at this crossing.

**River Mile 32** Stilling Basin below Lake Georgetown. Go downstream for wade fishing. This is stocked periodically in the winter with rainbows by the state. Turn left on Booty's Road off FM 2338 or the Andice Road and follow the road to the basin.

### San Gabriel River

**River Mile 0** Turn off Austin Avenue onto Morrow Street just north of the north fork crossing to access the San Gabriel city park. Drive to the lower end of the park and wade downstream for some good sunfish fishing and bass up to one and a half pounds. There is also a small lake in the park.

**River Mile 7** This is the CR 100 crossing of the river. CR 100 is off SH 29 east of Georgetown. This is called Mankin's Crossing. A canoe or float tube would be necessary above the crossing. The area below is wadeable but tends to be shallow.

**River Mile 10** This is the FM 1660 crossing at Jonah, Texas. Access is very poor, and this crossing is not recommended.

**River Mile 15** This is the CR 366 crossing off SH 29 west of Circleville. There are very steep banks, but one could wade above and use a boat below. Good take-out for float from CR 100.

**River Mile 18** This is the SH 95 crossing at Circleville. A road leads to the river on the southeast side of the bridge. This has good potential for a float from the CR 366 crossing of about 3 miles.

The water quality deteriorates very rapidly beyond this crossing.

## Food & Lodging on the San Gabriel

Nice motels in Georgetown include the Comfort Inn, 512-863-7504; the Georgetown Inn, 512-863-5572; and the Ramada Inn, 512-869-2541. The Page House is the only bed and breakfast listed. Their number is 512-863-8979. Camping in the Georgetown area includes the Cedar Breaks Park and Jim Hogg Park on Lake Georgetown, or the Tejas

Park on the North San Gabriel. Call 512-863-3016. Good restaurants include the Walberg Mercantile Restaurant in Walberg, Texas, which has excellent German food, and Bob's Catfish-N-More and The Egg Roll King in Georgetown.

# San Marcos River

FOUND ON PAGES 118 AND 130 OF THE ROADS OF TEXAS

Anyone reading about these rivers should be aware that some are easily waded, examples being the Nueces and the Llano, while others are best fished with a boat. The San Marcos falls into the latter category. The Blanco and the Frio would join the San Marcos due to potential for a confrontation with accusations about trespass while wading.

The San Marcos is deep, and its bottom tends to be unstable. There are multiple open-access points, but the majority of these are best left to bait fishermen. To get to the large bass and sunfish found on this river, therefore, you need some type of flotation. Be aware that there are three dams that require portage and three rapids that could be dangerous. You can get a good map of the river at Shady Grove Campground (see River Mile 10 below).

**River Mile 0** In Hays County, there are multiple roads in the city of San Marcos that cross the river and offer potential access. In addition, there is a boat ramp in the San Marcos City Park. There is a dam between this point and the next access.

**River Mile 5** Between Guadalupe and Caldwell counties, CR 101 crosses the river south of town. This road runs between FM 621 and SH 80. Good access with parking.

**River Mile 10** In Caldwell County, FM 1979 crosses the river west of Martindale, Texas. There is 100 yards of public access along the road right-of-way. This is a good take-out or launch site. Best access is on the south end of the bridge at Shady Grove Campground. The campground (512-327-6113) offers overnight camping, day use, canoe rentals, and shuttle service.

**River Mile 15.5** In Guadalupe County, FM 1977 crosses the river east of Staples, Texas. Staples is on FM 621. There is 100 yards of shoreline available. A dam just below the crossing will require a portage if you are floating downstream.

**River Mile 23** This is the FM 20 crossing of the river west of Fentress, Texas. This is in Caldwell County. Fentress is on SH 80 south of San Marcos. There is about 75 yards of public access along the road right-of-way.

**River Mile 26** This is a country road that crosses the river west of Prairie Lea, Texas. This is in Caldwell County. The road, marked "River," turns west off SH 80 1 block north of Black's Grocery.

**River Mile 28** This is the CR 116 crossing west of SH 80. Turn west; there is 30 yards of shoreline access along the road right-of-way.

**River Mile 29** This is the CR 119 crossing in Caldwell County west of Stairtown, Texas. There is a new bridge, and good access is available only on the southwest corner of the bridge.

**River Mile 35**  US 90 crosses the river west of Luling, Texas. There is about 100 yards of shoreline available for access. A roadside park is available for parking; the entrance is 8/10 mile from the bridge on the north side.

**River Mile 41.5**  This is at Luling City Park, off US 80 south of town. There is 1/2 mile of public access along the shoreline. This is in Caldwell County. Some camping facilities are available.

## Food & Lodging on the San Marcos

There is no public camping available in San Marcos. The better motels include Days Inn, 800-325-2525; Holiday Inn, 512-353-8011; and the Econolodge, 800-782-7653, ext. 182. The bed and breakfasts include the Crystal River Inn, 512-396-3739, and the Westover Bed and Breakfast at 512-396-8323. In addition to Shady Grove Campground (see Mile 10 above) there is Pecan Park Retreat (512-392-6171), a nice campground located near the Mile 5 crossing. The proprietors of the campground are Tom and Paula Goynes. Tom Goynes is currently president of the Texas Rivers Protection Association, a non-profit organization made up of pro-river activists from across the state representing landowner coalitions, conservationists, canoe clubs, and fishing associations. You can get membership information by writing to Goynes at Box 219, Martindale, Texas 78655. (Goynes also offers guided canoe trips down the San Marcos—he paddles, you fish.) Local restaurants recommended include Palmer's Restaurant and Bar and Fuschak's Pit Bar-B-Q. Herbert's Restaurant also comes highly recommended by local canoers.

# San Saba River

FOUND ON PAGES 99 AND 100 OF THE ROADS OF TEXAS

The San Saba River arises west of Fort McKavett in Schleicher County and flows east through Menard, Mason, and McCullough counties. This is a pretty stream but tends to be less clear than the Llano River. Access is a real problem. About twenty years ago there were ten fishing camps on the river between Menard and San Saba. Now there are none I have been able to find. Most of the road crossings are fenced or posted. Is this a harbinger of the future?

**River Mile 0** In Menard County, the first access available is a country road just east of Dry Creek off Highway 190 west of Menard. There is a huge hole above the crossing and good wade fishing below. This is a good launch site for a float to the Menard Country Club or Menard City Park.

**River Mile 8** This is the Menard Country Club and the site of the Presidio of the San Saba Mission. The Presidio is worth a visit by itself. This is a potential take-out point only but would require permission from the club manager.

**River Mile 9.5** City park in Menard. Access is good, but the river is deep and some type of flotation would be advised. This is a good take-out point or launch site.

**River Mile 14.5** This is the FM 2092 crossing 4 1/2 miles east of Menard. This would be a very good take-out point.

**River Mile 22** This is the second river crossing by FM 2092 about 9 1/2 miles east of Menard. A float tube, canoe, or boat could be used in the hole above the crossing. The river is fenced on both sides below. This is a good take-out point for a float from the previous crossing. This is about 7 1/2 river miles.

**River Mile 47** The next access point and the only remaining good access on the entire river is the crossing of US 87 south of Brady. There is a roadside park that gives access to the river. A large pool below would be ideal for a float tube, and one could use a canoe above or below the crossing. Some wade fishing is available, but a flotation device would give the best results. There are some huge sunfish here.

## Food & Lodging on the San Saba

In Menard, the Navaho Inn Restaurant is quite good. The Gonzales Restaurant is also recommended. The Navaho Inn, 915-396-4532, is a very nice motel. Tell Phil Barnes and his father "Hello" for us.

In Brady, Texas, the Sunset Inn, 915-597-0789, and the Plateau Motel,

915-597-2185, are nice and comfortable. A new motel, the Brady Inn, is under construction. Camping is available in Brady at Richard's Park and the Rocking R Ranch, 915-597-1866. Restaurants include the Texas Corral, Luigi's Italian Food, El Flamingo Mexican Restaurant, Pizza Hut, and The Cafe on the Square, which is only open for lunch.

# Fly-Fishing Outfitters in Texas

## AUSTIN

The Austin Angler, 312 1/2 Congress Avenue, (512) 472-4553

## DALLAS

Backwoods, 5500 Greenville Ave., #308, (214) 363-0372

Hunter Bradlee Co., 8314 Preston Center Plaza, (214) 363-9213

Orvis, 10720 Preston Road, (214) 265-1600

Westbank Anglers, Inwood Village, 5370 Lover's Lane #320
(214) 350-4665  FAX 350-4667

## FT. WORTH

Backwoods, 3212 Camp Bowie Boulevard, (817) 332-2423

## HOUSTON

The Angler's Edge, 3926 Westheimer, in Highland Village,
(713) 993-9981  FAX 993-9972

Cut Rate Fishing Tackle Unlimited
8933 Katy Freeway, (713) 827-7762

Orvis, 5848 Westheimer Road, (713) 783-2111

## NEW BRAUNFELS

Gruene Outfitters, 1629 Hunter Road, (210) 625-4440

## SAN ANTONIO

The Tackle Box Outfitters,
6330 N. New Braunfels, in Sunset Ridge Center,
(210) 821-5806